HYSTERICAL HISTORICAL FACTS AND JOKES

First published 2016 by Nosy Crow Ltd
The Crow's Nest, 14 Baden Place, Crosby Row
London SE1 1YW

www.nosycrow.com

ISBN 978 0 85763 619 5

Nosy Crow and associated logos are trademarks
and/or registered trademarks of Nosy Crow Ltd

A CIP catalogue record for this book is available from the British Library.

Printed and bound in the UK by Clays Ltd, St Ives Plc.

Papers used by Nosy Crow are made from wood grown in
sustainable forests.

3 5 7 9 8 6 4

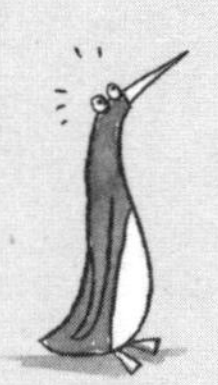

HEH
HEH!
HARRY THE HISTORY HOUND'S
HYSTERICAL
HISTORICAL
FACTS
AND JOKES
TRACEY TURNER
ILLUSTRATED BY SARAH HORNE

What do you get if you cross Henry V's fool with a football team?

Mad Jester United.

What do you call a knight who likes jousting?

Sir Lance-alot.

Why did knights swap places with one another before a tournament?

It was the knight shift.

STINKY FACT
In Victorian times, 'pure collectors' gathered dog poo from the streets. They sold it to tanners, who used it in the horrible and smelly leather-making process.

What did the pirate say when his wooden leg got stuck in Arctic ice?

'Shiver me timbers!'

Who invented fire?

Some bright spark.

What did Henry VIII become on his 21st birthday?

A year older.

Which skinny grandson of James VII tried to become king of Britain?

Boney Prince Charlie.

PUTRID PLAGUE FACT

There were plenty of revolting cures for the Black Death, the plague that struck Britain in 1348. One was to strap a live chicken to a plague sore.

When did early people become more smartly dressed?

In the Iron Age.

What is the favourite theme park ride of Anne Boleyn's ghost?

The rollerghoster.

FATAL FACT

The Earl of Huntly led a rebellion against Mary Queen of Scots. His rebellion was defeated and he was killed in battle, but Mary wanted his land, and the only way to get it was to have the Earl convicted of treason. So the Earl's body was put on trial, found guilty and beheaded.

What do you get if you cross a knight with a vampire?

A bite in shining armour.

Which inventor caused a revolution?

The inventor of the wheel.

Why did Robin Hood only steal from the rich?

Because the poor didn't have anything worth stealing.

Why did Captain Hook cross the road?

To get to the second-hand shop.

FOUL FACT

Ugh, I feel a bit ruff!

In the Middle Ages, castle toilets emptied into the moat or a toilet pit. People kept their clothes in toilets because the smell kept moths away.

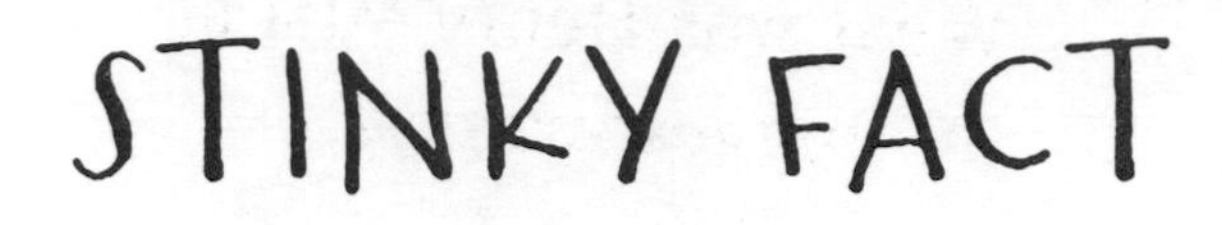

The smell of sewage in the River Thames was so bad during the hot summer of 1858 that it became known as the Great Stink. Sheets dipped in powerful chemicals were hung at the windows of the House of Commons to keep out the terrible whiff.

What was Henry VIII's biggest worry?

His receding heir line.

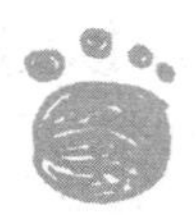

Where did knights go to eat their dinner?

An all-knight diner.

Which knight was always playing practical jokes?
Sir Prize.
Where were all the Kings and Queens of England crowned?
On the head.

FATAL FACT

In 1952, London fog mixed with sooty pollution made motorists abandon their cars and cows drop dead at Smithfield Market. The city came to a standstill and thousands of people died from breathing the polluted air.

What do you call a Norman knight armed with a sword and a mace?

Whatever he tells you to.

In the Middle Ages, most people used a chamber pot instead of a toilet. People emptied the pots out of the window into the street, calling 'Gardy loo!' to warn passers-by – 'gardy loo' comes from the French words 'regardez l'eau' ('mind the water') and it's where the word 'loo' comes from.

What do Queen Victoria and the Prince of Wales have in common?

They were both named after pubs.

What do you get if you cross a knight with a ghost?

A sprite in shining armour.

What do you call a very young army?

The infantry.

What do kings and queens do when they burp?

They issue a royal pardon.

PUTRID PLAGUE FACT

Tudor plague doctors dressed in a mask with a long beak stuffed with dried flowers and herbs, and doused their clothes in vinegar to ward off infection.

FOUL FOOD FACT

Victorian scientist William Buckland liked eating unusual food, including panther, mice on toast, owls, moles, and bluebottles (which he said tasted terrible). At a dinner party he was shown the embalmed heart of Louis XIV of France, and couldn't resist wolfing it down.

And they say dogs will eat anything!

Which king of Scotland could fly?

Robert the Goose.

Why did the pirate put a belt around a pumpkin?

He was a squash-buckler.

At the cinema a girl sees an old lady wearing a crown sitting in the seat next to her. 'Good grief! Are you Queen Victoria?' she asks. 'Yes,' the woman replies. 'What on earth are you doing here?' the girl asks. Queen Victoria replies, 'Well, I liked the book.'

What did King Richard II say when he heard there had been a rebellion by the common people?

'That was a peasant surprise.'

What do you call a pirate's parrot that's lost its memory?

Polynesia.

What was round, brown and shiny and fought at the Battle of Hastings?

William the Conker.

Two separate people claim to own the house where Shakespeare wrote Romeo and Juliet. They should just put a plaque on both their houses.

Another 'cure' for the Black Death was to bend over a toilet pit or drain (or anything that smells terrible) and take some deep breaths to drive away the disease.

Even I think that's disgusting . . . and I sniff other dog's bottoms!

FUNNY FACT

Queen Victoria's son accidentally shot his brother-in-law during a hunting trip. The brother-in-law, Prince Christian, lost an eye, and assembled a huge collection of glass ones that he liked to show people at parties – his favourite was a bloodshot eye.

What did people wear at the time of the Great Fire of London?

Blazers and smoking jackets.

Where is Hadrian's Wall?

Around Hadrian's garden.

Which Elizabethan explorer was also a baker?

Sir Francis Cake.

Why did the double-agent spy chicken cross the road, jump in a muddy ditch and cross back over the road again?

Because he was a dirty double-crosser.

People stand up for royalty . . .
But kings and queens sit down for royal tea.

Tee, hee!

Why did George I go to the dentist?

To have his teeth crowned.

What's as big as a pirate ship but weighs nothing?

Its shadow.

Why was the poet John Keats in trouble with the bank?

Because he Ode so much.

FOUL FOOD FACT

Rich people living in Tudor times ate unusual or spectacular foods to impress their guests: peacocks or swans, chickens stuffed inside pigs, or live birds inside pie crusts so that they'd fly out when the pastry case was cut open.

FUNNY FACT

A knight presented his king with a treasure trove of gold and jewels. 'Goodly knight, tell me of your noble deeds,' said the king. 'I've defeated your enemies to the east, and looted their villages,' said the knight. 'But I have no enemies in the east!' exclaimed the king. 'Well,' said the knight, 'you do now.'

Why were the Middle Ages so much fun?

Because of the knight life.

Which type of music was invented in the Stone Age?

Rock music.

Why is history a fruity subject?

Because it has so many dates.

What do you get if you cross a mad British king with a shark?

King Jaws III.

PLUNDERING PIRATE FACT

Blackbeard was amazed to discover one of his pirate crew playing chess with his parrot. 'Arrrr!' he exclaimed. 'That must be the cleverest parrot in all the seven seas!' 'Not really,' said the pirate. 'I've beaten him in three games out of five.'

Which knight never won a single battle?

Sir Endor.

Where did you dig that one up?

Why did Queen Anne keep drawing straight lines?

Because she was a ruler.

What does Nelson's Column stand for?

Because it can't sit down.

What do you call a pirate's lost parrot?

A polygon.

Why was the ghost of Anne Boleyn always running?

Because she wanted to get ahead.

FESTERING FACT

'Gong farmers' had one of the worst jobs in history: they cleared away waste in toilet pits before flushing toilets were invented. They had to dig out the pits and haul the liquid and solid waste away, under cover of darkness because no one wanted to see (or smell) them about their business.

Why do history teachers like fruit cake?

Because it's full of dates.

Why was the student's history essay wet?

Because her grade was below C level.

FATAL FACT

In 1867, the Reverend Thomas Baker was trying to spread the Christian religion to the Fiji islanders when he upset a Fijian chief. The islanders killed, cooked and ate the reverend and seven of his followers. In an elaborate ceremony in 2003, Fijians descended from Reverend Baker's killers apologised to the reverend's descendants for eating their ancestor.

What do you call Victorian ants?

Antiques.

Why were Richard I's troops too tired to fight?

They'd had lots of sleepless knights.

Who was Edward the Black Prince's father?

Old King Coal.

FOUL FOOD FACT

During and after the Second World War, food had to be rationed in Britain. Rook pie and squirrel tail soup appeared in wartime rationing cook books.

What's purple and burns?

The Grape Fire of London.

FUNNY FACT

A Tudor cure for the infectious disease smallpox was to hang red curtains around the patient's bed.

Bonkers books:

What did Richard the Lionheart listen to every night at ten o'clock?

The knightly news.

Why were the Middle Ages so dark?

Because there were so many knights.

FREAKY FACT

Some people were afraid of the effects of poisonous gases in the tail of Halley's comet when it passed the Earth in 1910, and bought anti-comet pills, gas masks, and anti-comet umbrellas.

PAINFUL FACT

Whacking pupils with a cane was considered an important part of education, but royal princes couldn't be hit by their teachers for doing something wrong. Instead a 'whipping boy', usually the son of a friend of the king, had to suffer the punishment for him.

What's my favourite Tudor accessory? The **ruff-ruff**!

How did Guy Fawkes get the idea for the Gunpowder Plot?

It just came to him in a flash.

Why doesn't the ghost of Anne Boleyn go to parties?

She has no body to go with.

FUNNY FOOD FACT

Welsh pirate Henry Morgan and his crew were stranded in 1670, and ended up cooking and eating leather shoes and satchels when they ran out of food.

Who was the first underwater spy?

James Pond.

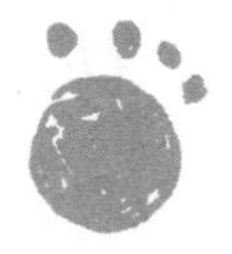

Did you hear about the inventor of the drill bit?

He created a real turning point.

Which one of Henry VIII's wives liked cricket?

Anne Boleyn.

Why did the student eat his history homework?

The teacher told him it was a piece of cake.

STRANGE FOOD FACT

Charles Darwin, the Victorian scientist with the theory about evolution, was a member of his university's Glutton Club, which met to eat unusual animals such as hawks and bitterns. On his round-the-world voyage, Darwin ate a rare flightless bird in South America and giant tortoises on the Galapagos Islands, and drank the contents of the tortoises' bladders.

FREAKY FACT

At the beginning of the 20th century, the 'S bend' was a fashion for women. Special underwear pushed the woman's top half forwards and her back half backwards, making an uncomfortable curved shape. Women sometimes had to lean on parasols for balance.

Why did the spy spend the Second World War in bed?

She was an undercover agent.

Knock-knock.

Who's there?

The interrupting pirate.

The interrup—

Arrrrrr!

FOUL FACT

In the Middle Ages, a cure for bad breath caused by a decayed tooth was to rub the tooth with powdered deer antler.

Why was the pirate so good at boxing?

Because of his powerful left hook.

Which king of England was round and purple?

Alfred the Grape.

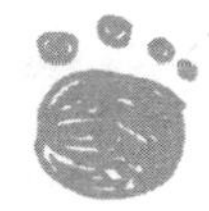

What has eight eyes and eight legs?

Eight pirates

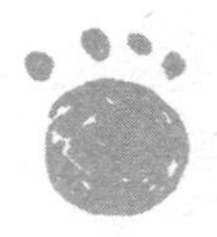

Where did knights take sick horses?

To the horsepital.

Why is the ghost of Mary Queen of Scots so bad at lying?

You can see right through her.

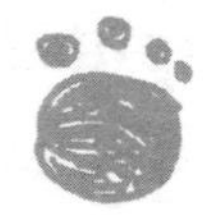

Who invented fractions?

Henry the Eighth.

STRANGE FACT

Naval hero Admiral Nelson was made of stern stuff. When his arm was shattered by a musket shot in battle, he had the arm amputated by a surgeon and was back on deck in command of his ship within half an hour.

STRANGE FACT

English Civil War leader Oliver Cromwell's body was dug up, hanged and beheaded when Cromwell fell out of favour two years after his death in 1660. The head went on a 300-year-long adventure of its own. It was displayed on a pole for 24 years, then blew off in a gale. It spent some time in a museum and in a travelling fair, until it was finally buried in 1960 at Cromwell's old college in Cambridge University.

How do archaeologists get into locked tombs?

They use a skeleton key.

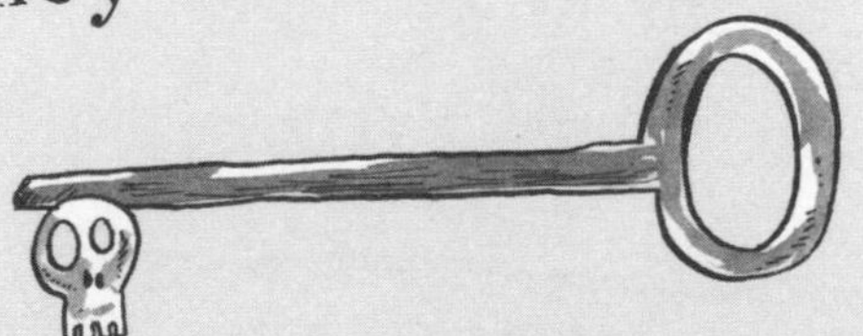

What name did Queen Elizabeth I give to her favourite chef when she made him a knight?

Sir Loin.

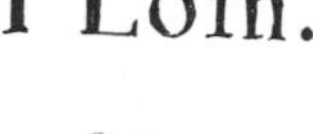

What do you call an angry pirate skeleton?

A skull and cross bones.

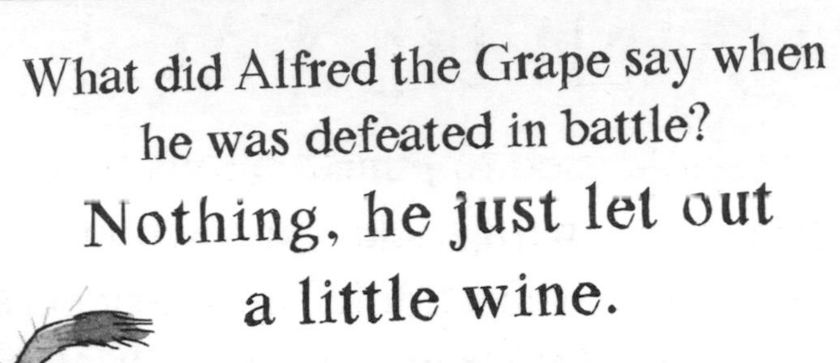

What did Alfred the Grape say when he was defeated in battle?

Nothing, he just let out a little wine.

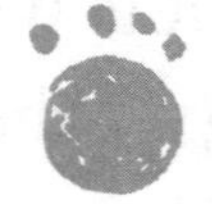

Where did medieval knights learn how to joust?

At knight school.

That's given me paws for thought!

What should you carve on a knight's gravestone?

PAINFUL FACT

Schools used to punish pupils by hitting them with sticks. At a school in Cambridge in the Middle Ages, teachers showed off their whacking skills at the beginning of the school year by demonstrating on local children.

CURIOUS CURES

To cure a sore throat in medieval times you might tie a string of worms around your neck – the idea was that as the worms died, the sore throat went away.

Which Scottish king had the biggest crown?

The one with the biggest head.

Why was the archaeologist upset?

Because his career was in ruins.

William Shakespeare asked his friend if he should stop writing plays and concentrate on his poetry instead.

'No,' said his mate, 'that would be going from bard to verse.'

What does HMS Victory have in common with a shopaholic?

They're both driven by sales.

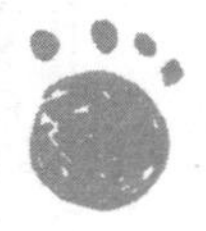

In which famous battle were there desperate queues for the toilet?

The Battle of Portaloo.

FUNNY FACT

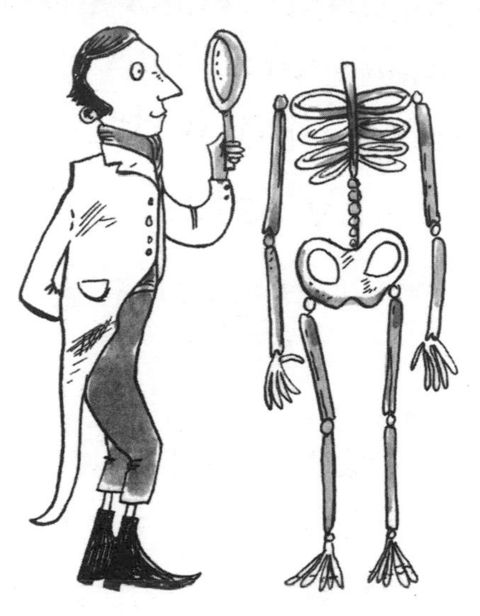

Royal Surgeon Henry Halford was asked to examine the skeleton of Charles I (who'd been executed in the Civil War in 1649). Halford secretly stole one of Charles I's bones, and liked to shock people at dinner parties by using it as a salt cellar. Years later, Queen Victoria found out about it and ordered Halford to return the bone to the dead king's skeleton.

Why are pirates called pirates?

They just arrrrrrr.

Why did the ghost of Anne Boleyn cross the road?

To get to the Other Side.

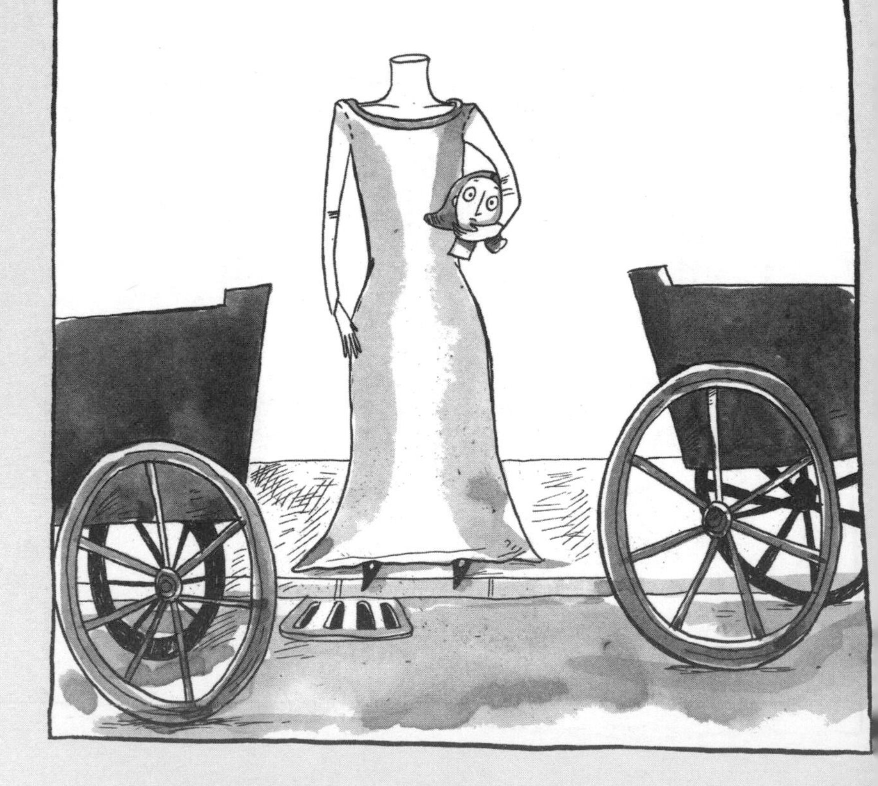

What do you call a knight who swears?

Sir Cuss.

Why did King Harold ride his horse into the Battle of Hastings?

It was too heavy to carry.

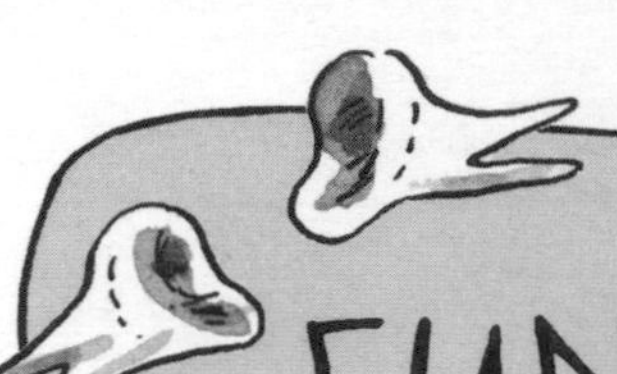

Medieval barber-surgeons were hairdressers, dentists and doctors. They might pull out a tooth (one of the only cures for toothache), open someone's vein to let out blood (which was the 'cure' for lots of different ailments), then trim a man's beard, all in a day's work.

What do you call a really ancient joke?

Pre-hysterical.

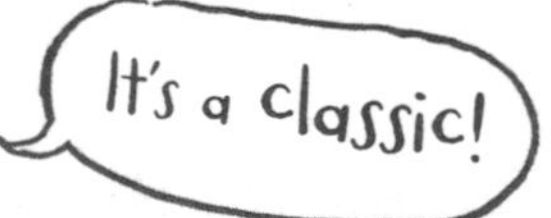

When did Queen Victoria get very wet?

When she became the reigning monarch.

Which one of Shakespeare's plays is about a small gammon steak?

Hamlet.

Which pirate told the most jokes?

Captain Kidd.

Why did the student miss his history class?

He got the date wrong.

PUTRID PLAGUE FACT

Because foul smells were thought to keep the Black Death at bay, some people farted into a bottle and then corked the bottle, so that they'd always have a bad smell handy.

Did you know the Great Fire of London started in a bakery?

Afterwards the business was toast.

FUNNY FACT

Charles Babbage invented the world's first mechanical computer in the 19th century. But when he was a teenager he nearly drowned trying out shoes he'd invented to walk on water.

The castle defenders were wondering why the cannonball seemed to be getting bigger and bigger . . .

Then it hit them.

Which ghost haunts the Houses of Parliament?

The Spooker of the House.

Why was the ghost of Mary Queen of Scots friendly with the demons?

Because demons are a ghoul's best friend.

Over a tot of rum in a tavern, a man gets talking to a pirate with a peg leg, a hook and an eyepatch. 'How did you lose your leg?' the man asks the pirate. 'Arrr,' says the pirate, ''twas bitten off by a shark in Dead Man's Cove.' The man gives a shudder. 'And your hand?' he asks. 'Arrrr. Chopped off in a sword fight,' replies the pirate. 'Nasty,' says the man. 'What about your eye?' 'Seagull poo,' says the pirate. The man looks puzzled. 'Arrr,' says the pirate, ''twas my first day with the hook.'

What were King Harold's last words at the Battle of Hastings?

'I spy with my little eye something beginning with A.'

What do you call a knight who used to be a doctor?

Sir Jen.

What did the pirate get when he crossed his parrot with a shark?

A parrot that talked his ear off.

Why did it take pirates ages to learn the alphabet?

Because they spent so long at C.

Who made the Round Table for King Arthur?

Sir Cumference.

What about the hound table?

Why were medieval prisoners
like blacksmiths?

They would sometimes
make a bolt for the door.

Where did King John sign
the Magna Carta?

At the bottom.

Why did Captain Cook sail
to Australia?

It was too far to swim.

A medieval cure for deafness was to leave a dead eel to rot in horse manure, then stick the rotten eel in your ear.

What kind of shoes did spies wear in the Second World War?

Sneakers.

What did the egg in the monastery say?

'Out of the frying pan, into the friar.'

What was the most striking achievement of Victorian times?

The invention of matches.

Why did the knight have to leave the archery competition?

He found it too 'arrowing.

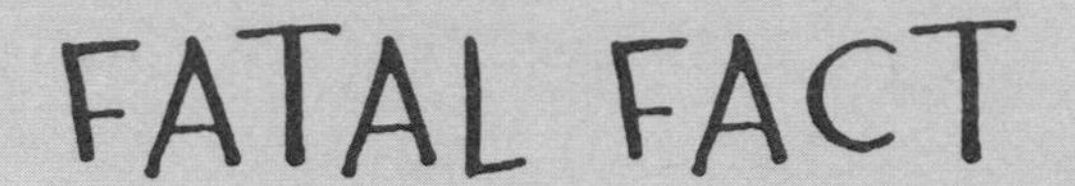

In the Middle Ages, aggressive pigs could be dangerous to people. A pig that had killed someone would stand trial, with a lawyer to defend it, and if found guilty it would be sentenced to death, usually by hanging.

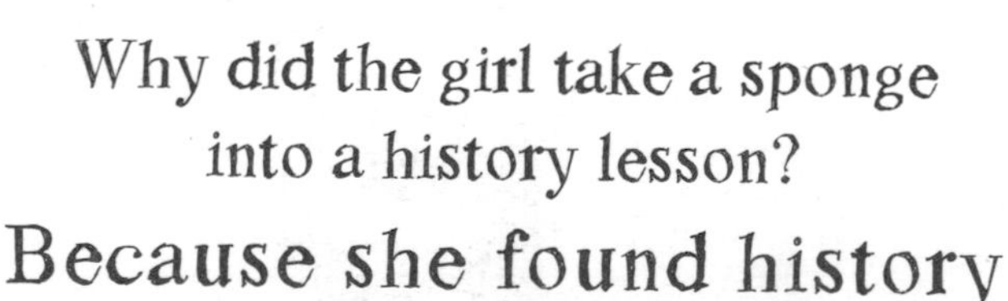

Why did the girl take a sponge into a history lesson?

Because she found history such an absorbing subject.

What's cleverer than a pirate's talking parrot?

A spelling bee.

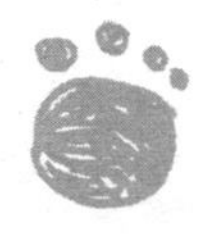

What did Henry II say when he found out his sons were plotting against him?

'I'm having a bad heir day.'

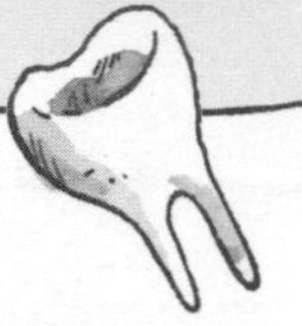

PAINFUL FACT

In the Middle Ages, often the only cure for toothache was having the tooth pulled out. For painless extraction, a book recommended burning newts and beetles and grinding them into a powder, then rubbing the powder onto the tooth.

Why did the pirate blush?

Because the seaweed.

What was crusading King Richard the Lionheart's favourite game?

Knights and crosses.

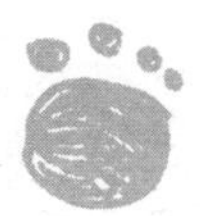

Which English king invented the fireplace?

Alfred the Grate.

Where were traitors beheaded in medieval London?

Just above the shoulders.

Why did King Arthur have a round table?

So no one could corner him.

STRANGE FACT

In the 1700s, the Countess of Eglinton kept tame rats, which ran free about her mansion. The rats scurried to the dining table when the Countess called them, then scampered off again when she told them to.

What was Alexander Graham Bell's brother's name?

Ding Dong.

PAINFUL FACT

If you killed or injured someone in Saxon times you had to pay money to the victim's family – 200 shillings for killing a peasant, 30 shillings if you chopped off his ear, or 60 shillings for chopping off his nose.

Why is there no point in becoming a historian?

There's no future in it.

What's a snake's favourite subject?

Hissstory.

Which knight designed
Egyptian tombs?

Sir Cophagus.

I might die of
laughter!

STRANGE FACT

Georgian make-up included poisonous lead paint and arsenic powder. Georgian women put balls made of chalk inside their cheeks because they thought it was a good look.

Why was Elizabeth I buried at Westminster Abbey?

Because she was dead.

What do William the Conqueror and Peter the Great have in common?

They both have the same middle name.

Why did the history teacher never teach his class about the Iron Age?

He was too rusty on the subject.

KILL OR CURE?

In Tudor times, teething babies were sometimes given a horse's tooth to chew on. Or they might have a mixture made from hare's brains, goose fat and honey rubbed on their gums.

Which Elizabethan explorer could stop traffic?

Sir Francis Brake.

Which 18th-century explorer was eaten by cannibals?

Captain Cooked.

What happened when pirates attacked a ship carrying blue and red paint?

The crew was marooned.

FOUL FACT

The explorer Walter Raleigh was executed in 1618. His wife, Elizabeth Throckmorton, kept his head in a leather bag until she died 29 years later, then Raleigh's son looked after it until he died too, when he and his father's head were both buried.

Why was the knight's horse so negative?

It was always saying 'neigh'.

STRANGE FACT

The philosopher Jeremy Bentham died in 1832. As he'd wished, his body was dissected by students at University College, London, and afterwards his skeleton was padded out with straw, dressed in Bentham's clothes and put on display. Bentham had intended that his head should be mummifi ed and placed on top, but the process didn't work out very well, and a wax head was used instead. The wax head and padded skeleton is still on display at University College.

What do you get if you shrink a knight?

A mite in shining armour.

Why was the Prince Regent like a book?

Because he had so many pages.

Why was Henry II's fool always shrugging and raising his eyebrows?

He was the court gesture.

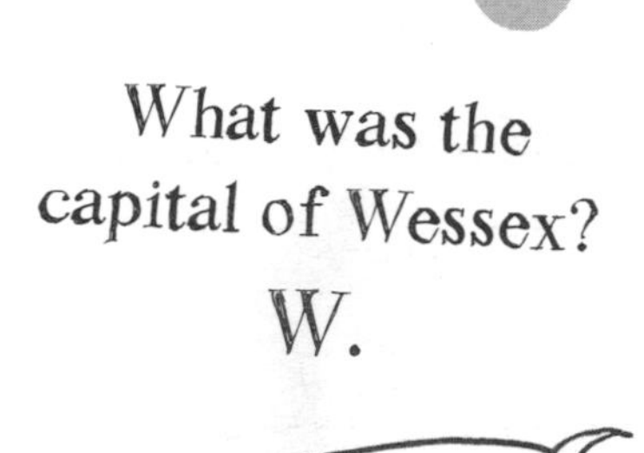

What was the capital of Wessex?

W.

How did crusading knights get down from camels?

They didn't. Down comes from geese.

What was Camelot famous for?

Its knight life.

STINKY FACT

Henry VIII had a Groom of the Stool, a highly paid aristocrat whose duties included wiping the king's bottom after he'd been to the toilet.

What happens to a usurped king or queen?

They're over-throne.

What's a knight's charger's favourite game?

Stable tennis.

STINKY FACT

Blue dye used to be made from the plant woad, and the dye-making process smelled absolutely terrible. It was so bad that Queen Elizabeth I made it a rule that there was to be no woad-dyeing within five miles of her royal person.

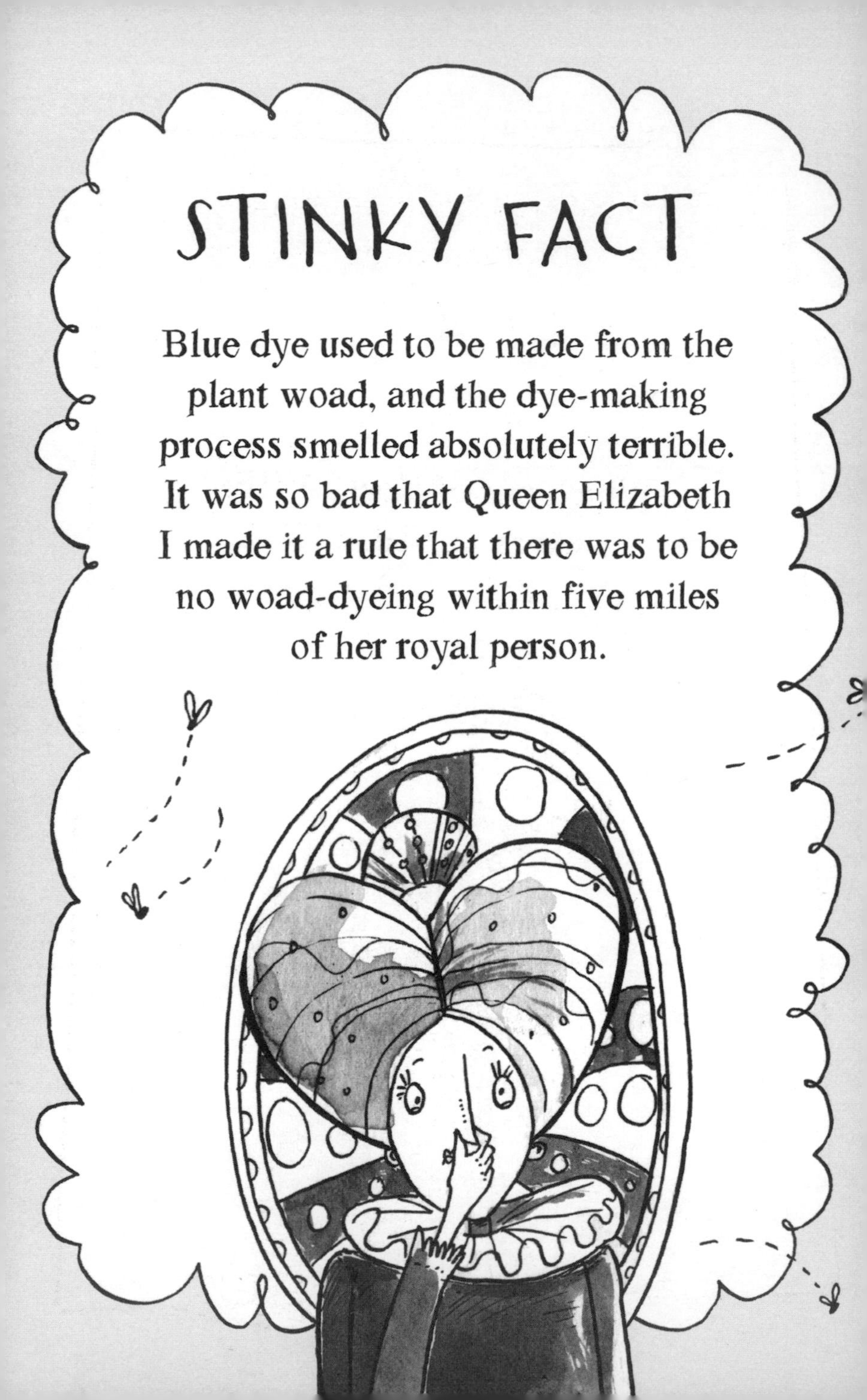

What was Anne Boleyn's brother called?

Tenpin.

Which one of Henry VIII's wives played golf?

Catherine Parr.

FUNNY FACT

In the 1400s, there was a fashion for shoes with such long, pointed toes that the points had to be reinforced with whalebone or tied to the leg to stop people tripping up when they walked.

What do history teachers do before they get married?

They go on dates.

What comes right in the middle of history?

The letter t.

Hee, hee!

What do you call a nervous prehistoric hunter?

Shakespeare.

How many pirates could you fit inside an empty Albert Hall?

One. After that, it wouldn't be empty any more.

King Charles II rubbed his body with dust from ancient Egyptian mummies, in the belief that it would make him a great king.

What do you call a knight who used to work as a butler?

Sir Vent.

What marks did the pirates get in their exams?

High Cs.

What do you call a soldier armed with a musket who has whiskers and a long tail?

A mouseketeer.

STINKY FACT

King Henry II of England employed a farting jester known as Roland the Farter. When Roland retired, he was given a huge house and land as a retirement present, but he still had to entertain the king on Christmas Day with his hilarious comedy routines. King John employed a French farting entertainer, Peter the Farter.

Why did the Second World War code-breaker spend so long in the orchestra?

He was looking for cymbals.

What do you call two knights' horses that live next door to one another?

Neigh-bours.

PLUNDERING PIRATE FACT

Blackbeard was an especially scary English pirate. When he was eventually captured by the English navy in 1718, he had to be shot and stabbed more than 20 times before he finally died (or so the story goes).

How did people get to know one another in the Stone Age?

By joining clubs.

Why did Henry VIII have so many wives?

He was always chopping and changing.

Why is Britain such a wet country?

Because kings and queens have been reigning there for centuries.

Where did medieval knights keep their camels?

Camelot.

What was the first thing Henry VIII did when he came to the throne?

He sat down.

What's another term for the Middle Ages?

Knight time.

FOUL FOOD FACT

At King James II's coronation banquet in 1685, 100 dishes were served, including cold puffin, stags' tongues , and trotter pie.

Why did no one play cards on HMS Victory?

Because Lord Nelson was standing on the deck.

What happened when King Canute threw a pebble into the sea?

It got wet.

Bit like when I ran into a poodle!

What happened when the ghost of Mary Queen of Scots got lost in the fog?

She was mist.

What's a pirate's favourite country?

Arrrrrgentina.

FUNNY ANIMAL FACT

King Henry III set up a zoo in the Tower of London, where he kept three leopards, a bear and an elephant. The polar bear was allowed to fish for its dinner in the River Thames.

PREPOSTEROUS PLAGUE FACT

Smoking tobacco – a plant that came from America – became popular with wealthy Tudor people because they thought it was healthy and would ward off the plague.

Which side of knights' horses had more hair?

The outside.

Where did Richard II keep his armies?

Up his sleevies.

What do you call a sunken pirate ship that shivers and shakes on the seabed?

A nervous wreck.

What was the name of the Scottish king who loved garlic and pickled onions?

Macbreath.

STINKY FACT
The Earl of Oxford accidentally farted while bowing to Queen Elizabeth I and was so embarrassed that he stayed away from court for seven years. When he came back, Queen Elizabeth saw him and burst out laughing, saying, 'I had forgot the fart!'
Parp!

Did you hear about the knight's charger that ate with its mouth open and dropped oats all over the floor?

It had terrible stable manners.

Why are there 32 letters in the pirate alphabet?

Because there are seven Cs.

Which Elizabethan explorer was a slippery character?

Sir Francis Snake.

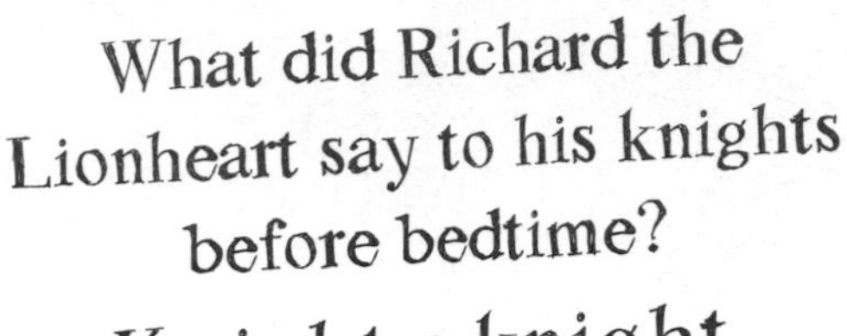

What did Richard the Lionheart say to his knights before bedtime?

Knighty-knight.

King John was almost hit in the chest at an archery tournament.

He had an arrow escape.

TOILET FACT

The first flushing toilet in Britain was invented by Elizabeth I's godson, John Harrington, in 1596. The Queen used it and ordered one for herself, but most people carried on using chamber pots.

What was a lady-in-waiting's favourite sport?

Tennis: they all served in the royal court.

How much did the pirate pay for his peg leg and hook?

An arm and a leg.

Why was the knight obsessed with his armour?

It was riveting.

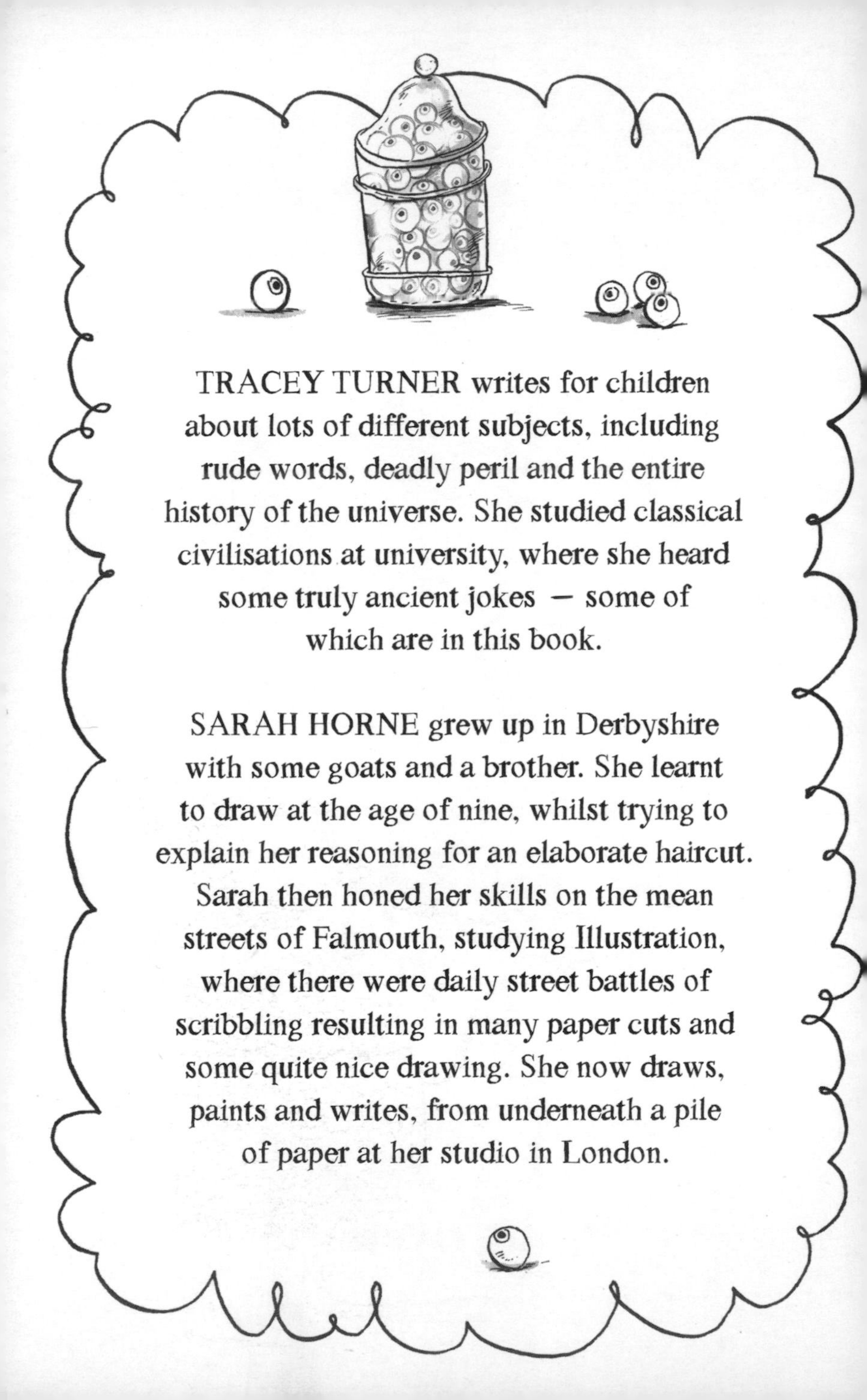

TRACEY TURNER writes for children about lots of different subjects, including rude words, deadly peril and the entire history of the universe. She studied classical civilisations at university, where she heard some truly ancient jokes – some of which are in this book.

SARAH HORNE grew up in Derbyshire with some goats and a brother. She learnt to draw at the age of nine, whilst trying to explain her reasoning for an elaborate haircut. Sarah then honed her skills on the mean streets of Falmouth, studying Illustration, where there were daily street battles of scribbling resulting in many paper cuts and some quite nice drawing. She now draws, paints and writes, from underneath a pile of paper at her studio in London.

That's all for now!
Time to take a
bow-wow!